GO FACTS TRANSPORT
Boats

A & C BLACK • LONDON

Boats

© Blake Publishing 2003
Additional material © A & C Black Publishers Ltd 2005

First published 2003 in Australia by Blake Education Pty Ltd

This edition published 2005 in the United Kingdom by
A & C Black Publishers Ltd, 37 Soho Square, London W1D 3QZ
www.acblack.com

ISBN-10: 0-7136-7271-4
ISBN-13: 978-0-7136-7271-8

A CIP record for this book is available from the British Library.

Written by Ian Rohr
Design and layout by The Modern Art Production Group
Photos by John Foxx, Photodisc, Corel, Corbis, Photo Alto, Brand X,
Digital Stock, Comstock and Eyewire.

UK series consultant: Julie Garnett

Printed in China by WKT Company Ltd.

A & C Black uses paper produced with elemental chlorine-free pulp,
harvested from managed sustainable forests.

Contents

What Is a Boat?

Boats carry people and things across water.

Boats come in many sizes. There are small boats such as canoes and large ships that can cross oceans.

Anchor

Boats have different uses. Cruise ships take people on holidays while other ships carry **cargo**. Yachts and sailboats are mainly used for fun. Ferries can take people to work or school.

Ships carry cargo around the world.

The largest cruise ships can carry more than 3000 people.

Sailboats are used for fun and racing.

Old Boats

People have made boats for thousands of years.

The first boats were simple canoes and rafts. Early canoes were carved from logs. People joined wooden or bamboo poles together to make rafts. They used **paddles** to move these boats.

Later, people built sailboats. Sails catch the wind and push the boat across the water. Sailboats are faster than boats with paddles.

Tall ships

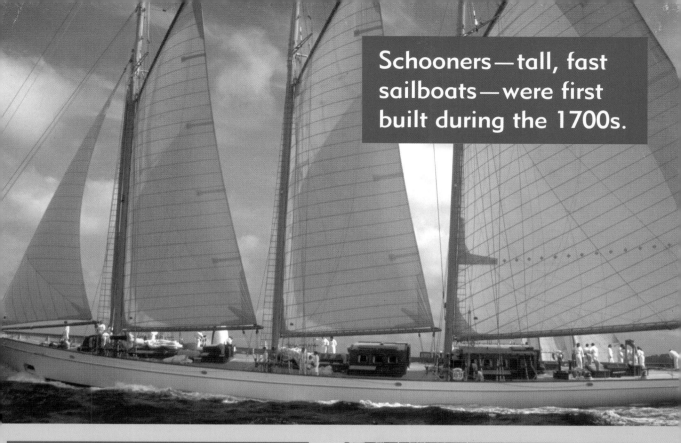

Schooners—tall, fast sailboats—were first built during the 1700s.

Rafts can float because they are made of wood which is lighter than water.

People have sold their goods out of boats for hundreds of years.

Many people use small boats for fishing or for fun.

Canoes today are narrow and light with pointed ends. People paddle canoes in shallow, quiet waters.

In row-boats, people use oars to push through the water. Row-boats are often used for fishing on calm rivers and lakes.

Speedboats have powerful engines and can travel very fast. Sometimes people waterski behind speedboats.

Speedboat

Lifeguards train in long row-boats.

Canoes are light enough to be carried over land or shallow water.

People in small boats should always wear life jackets.

9

Moving People

People travel short distances on ferries. Cruise ships can take you all the way around the world.

Ferries travel across rivers, **harbours** and lakes. Some people catch ferries to work or school. Larger ferries also travel between islands or even between countries.

Ferry

People take holidays on cruise ships. You live on the ship as it travels to different cities and countries. Cruise ships have restaurants, shops, cinemas and bedrooms called cabins.

In London small ferries take people across the river to work.

Ferries can be big enough to carry people and their cars.

Cruise ships have swimming pools and tennis courts.

Working Boats

Tankers, tugboats and barges are all working boats.

Cargo ships move goods such as cars, oil and food. Most goods are loaded onto ships in containers.

Oil tanker

Tugboats work in harbours. They are small but very strong. Tugboats tow or push ships in and out of harbours.

Barges are long, flat, slow boats. They **transport** heavy goods, such as logs and rubbish, along rivers and canals.

Tugs, barges and cargo ships work alongside one another at busy ports.

GO FACT!

BIGGEST!

The world's biggest ship is an oil tanker, the *Jahre Viking*. It is as long as five football fields.

Fishing boats are another kind of working boat.

The Navy

The navy is the seagoing part of the armed services.

Destroyer

Destroyers, submarines and aircraft carriers are all used by the navy.

Destroyers are fast. They are often used to protect bigger, slower ships.

Submarines can travel under the water when their tanks are full of water. To rise to the surface, the water is pushed out of the tanks by **compressed air**.

Aircraft carriers are the biggest ships in the navy. They carry planes which can take off and land on their long decks.

The biggest aircraft carriers can have 5000 sailors and pilots on board.

GO FACT!

DID YOU KNOW?

A U.S. submarine travelled around the world without surfacing. It took 12 weeks.

Submarines can hold up to 150 people.

A battleship fires its guns.

Glossary

cargo	goods that are moved by large vehicles
compressed air	air under pressure which takes up less space than air we breathe
destroyer	a small, fast warship
harbour	a protected body of water where boats are kept
paddle	a short oar
transport	move from one place to another

Index

16